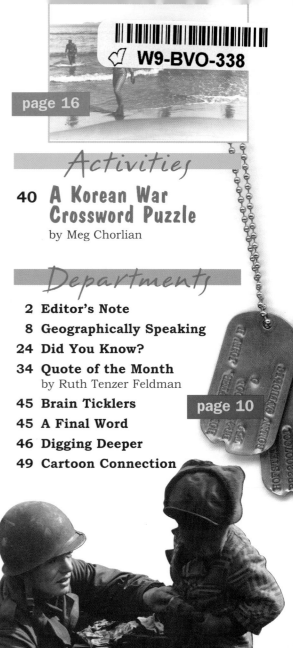

page 16

W9-BVO-338

page 10

page 26

Hey, Sis! Mom wants to know if you'll be home for dinner tonight!!

page 24

Editor's Note

For years, the Korean War (1950–1953) was known as the "Forgotten War." Coming on the heels of World War II (1941–1945) and followed quickly by the Vietnam War (1954–1973), the Korean War has often been overlooked by both historians and the American people.

The Korean War was fought during a time of great mistrust among nations. Onetime allies, the United States (a democratic nation) and the Soviet Union (a communist nation) were at odds with each other after World War II. Their ideological differences led to a period of political tension and military rivalry

called the Cold War. Though technically at peace, both countries built up their military forces in anticipation of an armed conflict.

At the end of World War II, Korea was divided into two regions. North Korea was occupied by Soviet troops, South Korea by U.S. military personnel and advisors. Intended to be a temporary situation until a unified Korea could govern itself, divided Korea became a testing ground for the two superpowers. Neither one was willing to tolerate the spread of the other's political system. Both were committed to supporting any country that shared their own philosophy. By 1948, communist North Korea and democratic South Korea established independent governments rather than a single unifying one. Two years later, the Korean War began.

The year 2000 marks the fiftieth anniversary of the start of the Korean War. In this issue of *COBBLESTONE,* we focus on the history of this armed conflict — from the two years of peace talks, to the roles of women and African Americans in the war, to the relief work done on behalf of Korean refugees. By examining the most important elements of this war, we hope that young people will remember not only the war itself but also all those who served, fought, and died in it.

Meg Chorlian
Editor

The Korean War took a toll on soldiers and civilians. Despite differences in their cultures, ages, and perspectives, the expressions of war weariness on this soldier's face (ABOVE) and that of a Korean boy (OPPOSITE) are strikingly similar.

3

The last thing Americans wanted to think about in August 1945 was more fighting. World War II was at long last over. Even the most optimistic people, however, knew that the prospects for lasting peace were not good. By the time the war officially ended on September 2, 1945, the seeds of continuing conflict were already sown.

A deep mutual dislike between the United States and the Soviet Union (also known as the Union of Soviet Socialist Republics, or U.S.S.R.) divided East and West. Each distrusted the other as much as they had both distrusted Adolf Hitler's Germany during World War II. The United States was a capitalist democracy. The Soviet Union was a socialist and communist nation, the exact opposite of the United States economically and politically. The way each viewed itself and the world fed their differences.

Nevertheless, when Soviet and U.S. differences spilled over into a shooting war in Korea, it surprised almost everyone. The U.S. military clearly did not think Korea worth the cost. Most Americans had only a vague notion of where Korea was or why it might be important.

The Soviet Union, however, knew Korea well. The two countries shared a short border. The U.S.S.R. had encouraged and trained Korean resistance fighters in the North during the Japanese occupation of Korea that began in 1910. By helping Korea, the Soviets hoped to gain access to its warm-water seaports, rich mineral deposits, and highly developed industrial base in the North. This was one reason Soviet premier Joseph Stalin declared war on Japan in 1945.

In the closing days of World War II, Soviet troops entered Korea from the north. The closest American soldiers were hun-

WAR on

by Randy Krehbiel

Guns on the USS Iowa *bombard North Korea.*

dreds of miles away. Hastily, the United States drafted a plan calling for the U.S.S.R. to accept the surrender of Japanese forces north of the 38th Parallel, while the United States would do the same south of that latitude. Somewhat to the Americans' surprise, Stalin agreed.

The Allies had promised an independent and united Korea. The United States, however, had

the Horizon

A Marine runs across a valley in Okinawa, Japan, that came to be known as Death Valley because of the losses suffered there during World War II.

in mind an independent Korea unified under a democratic government. The U.S.S.R. wanted a unified communist country.

The United States proposed a four-nation trusteeship to govern Korea temporarily, but the Soviets, as well as many Koreans, opposed it. In September 1947, the United States asked the newly formed United Nations (UN) to settle the issue. The UN said that the Koreans themselves should form a *provisional* government. Once they did, all foreign troops should be withdrawn. A commission was established to observe and supervise the elections.

The Korean officials installed by the Soviets in the North refused to allow the elections. But on May 10, 1948, South Koreans elected two hundred representatives to the new national assembly of the Republic of Korea. Seats were left open for the North to fill.

Syngman Rhee, who had been exiled by the Japanese, was chosen president of South Korea. The United States supported Rhee, but he quickly proved troublesome. He was a poor administrator and alarmed the Americans with his threats against the North.

Meanwhile, a Soviet-sponsored government was set up in the North. The Democratic People's Republic of Korea was proclaimed in September 1948, with Kim Il Sung as premier.

The U.S.S.R. began withdrawing its troops, until by late 1948 it had only a few advisors remaining in North Korea. The United States began pulling out, too, and by early 1950 it had only five hundred military personnel in South Korea. The North Koreans, though, were much more heavily armed than their southern counterparts. The United States feared that Rhee might make good on his threats if it supplied him with tanks, heavy artillery, or planes.

Back in Washington, U.S. policy seemed confused. President Harry S. Truman promised in 1947 to help any nation fighting communism, but he was reluctant to commit armed forces to Korea. A secret government document written in 1948 said that the United States should provide military equipment and economic aid to South Korea but withdraw its troops as soon as possible. Congress criticized Truman for being "soft on communism" but turned aside administration requests for additional military aid to Rhee. In January 1950, Secretary of State Dean Acheson made a speech that did not include South Korea as a nation of vital interest to the United

Provisional means temporary.

States. Many people believe that this speech encouraged North Korea to *mobilize.* But Kim had already obtained Stalin's and communist Chinese leader Mao Zedong's permission to attack the South.

Stalin was worried about U.S. plans to build permanent military bases in Japan. He also was unhappy about the formation of the North Atlantic Treaty Organization (NATO), which had militarily united Western Europe and the United States. Embarrassing the United States in Korea, Stalin thought, would weaken the confidence of its allies and damage its credibility in the UN. Given the United States' apparent uncertainty, Stalin must have doubted its will to support the South Koreans.

Stalin agreed to Kim's invasion plan, based on his belief that the United States would not risk another war by defending South Korea. The United States inadvertently encouraged that belief because it thought Stalin would not risk a full-scale war by supporting an attack on the South. The Soviet Union and the United States had completely misread each other's intentions, and the consequences of this misunderstanding would be tragic.

Randy Krehbiel is a reporter for the newspaper *Tulsa World* and a contributor to *COBBLESTONE.*

> **Mobilize** means to prepare or put into action for war.

> *On May 10, 1948, South Koreans vote in the first democratic elections.*

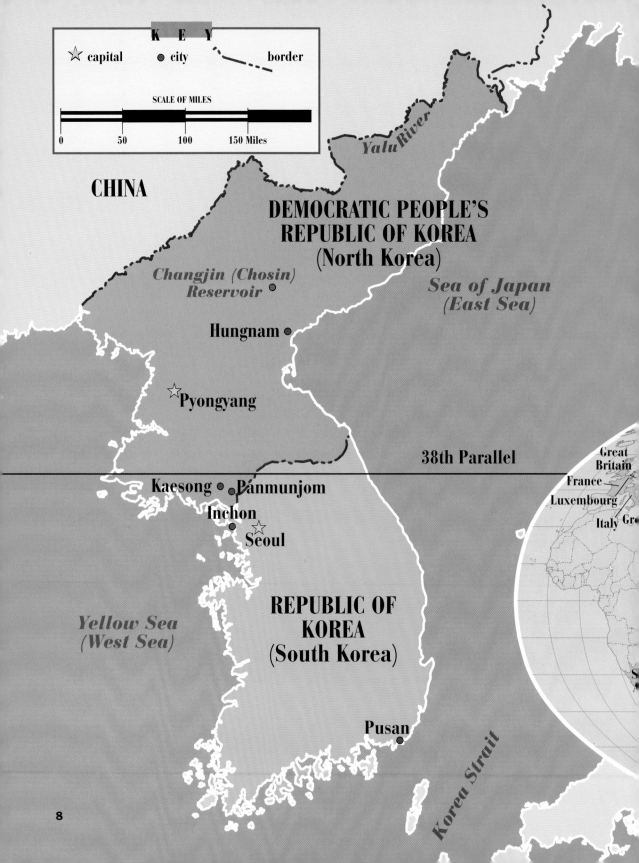

KEY

☆ capital   ● city   ·—·—· border

SCALE OF MILES

0   50   100   150 Miles

CHINA

Yalu River

DEMOCRATIC PEOPLE'S REPUBLIC OF KOREA (North Korea)

Changjin (Chosin) Reservoir

Sea of Japan (East Sea)

● Hungnam

☆ **Pyongyang**

38th Parallel

Kaesong ● ● Panmunjom

Inchon ●

☆ Seoul

Yellow Sea (West Sea)

REPUBLIC OF KOREA (South Korea)

Great Britain

France

Luxembourg

Italy   Gr

Pusan ●

Korea Strait

S

DIVIDED BY WAR
Korea and the World
1950–1953

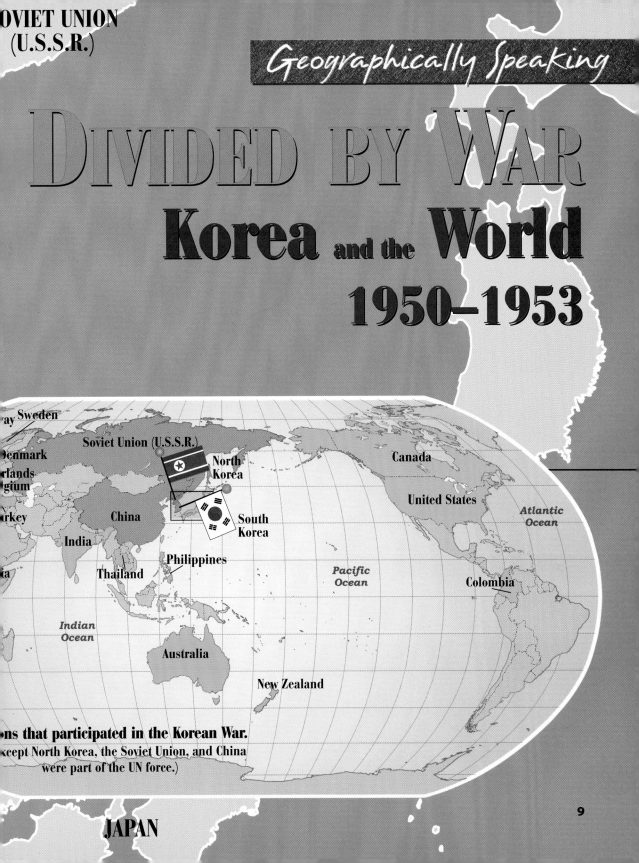

SOVIET UNION
(U.S.S.R.)

Sweden
Denmark
lands
gium
rkey
China
India
Thailand
Philippines
Soviet Union (U.S.S.R.)
North Korea
South Korea
Canada
United States
Atlantic Ocean
Pacific Ocean
Colombia
Indian Ocean
Australia
New Zealand
JAPAN

ns that participated in the Korean War.
cept North Korea, the Soviet Union, and China
were part of the UN force.)

9

THE Forgotten War

by Craig E. Blohm

S ince its creation, Korea has been known as the "Land of the Morning Calm." It is the English translation of Choson, the original name for Korea.

At 4:00 A.M. on June 25, 1950, that calm was shattered by the thunder of artillery shells exploding around Kaesong, the ancient Korean capital. North and South Korean troops had been sparring for months along the 38th Parallel, the dividing line between the two countries. Now North Korean combat troops were pouring across the border. Barely five years after World War II ended, the United States again found itself involved in a war halfway around the world.

Trained by Soviet officers, the North Korean army had 135,000 troops, plus artillery, combat planes, and 150 Soviet tanks. Against this force, the army of

American F-86 Sabre jets hunt for Soviet-built MiG-15s over North Korea. The place where MiGs were most often seen became known as MiG Alley, a common site of air battles in the spring of 1951.

the Republic of Korea (South Korea) could muster only 95,000 men. Because the United States feared that South Korean president Syngman Rhee might use military force against the North, it had purposely left his army under-equipped. It was not surprising, then, that soon after the invasion began, the South Korean army was on the run.

Interpreting North Korea's actions as "war against the United Nations," the UN Security Council held an emergency meeting on June 25. By a vote of 9 to 0, the Security Council agreed on a resolution to stop the North Koreans. On June 27, the UN also called on its member nations to help "restore international peace" in Korea.

By June 28, North Korean troops were poised to capture Seoul, the South Korean capital. As the South Korean army retreated, they planned to blow up bridges near the city to delay the enemy's advance. But in a tragic mistake, they destroyed the bridges too soon. Hundreds of refugees were killed, and soldiers and equipment were stranded in the enemy's path. Within hours, Seoul fell to the North Koreans.

When it became obvious that the South Korean army desperately needed help, U.S. president Harry S. Truman ordered American combat troops into Korea. On July 1, about four hundred soldiers of the 1st Battalion, 21st Infantry Regiment, 24th Infantry Division arrived in Pusan, a seaport on the southeast coast of Korea. Called Task Force Smith, the troops headed north to meet the invading North Korean army. These inexperienced soldiers fared no better than the South Koreans against the determined enemy. Encountering thousands of North Korean troops equipped with tanks and artillery, Task Force Smith was forced to retreat.

The UN then asked the United States to organize a multinational effort to carry out its objectives. One of those was "to repel the armed attack" of North Korea by providing military assistance. Truman agreed,

naming General Douglas MacArthur head of the UN command on July 10.

By the end of July, the North Korean army had overrun most of South Korea, pushing the UN forces south almost to the sea. In a last-ditch effort, UN forces established a ninety- by fifty-mile defensive area around Pusan. Within this "Pusan Perimeter," some 140,000 U.S. and South Korean troops were the last hope for saving South Korea. If the Pusan Perimeter fell, the war would be lost.

Meanwhile, MacArthur was devising a daring plan to retake South Korea. He would land an invasion force at Inchon, a port just west of Seoul. Landing troops there, behind the North Korean forces, would trap the enemy and cut off its supply lines and escape routes. MacArthur's superiors called his plan impossible. Underwater mines, thirty-foot tides, and steep sea walls would make such a landing extremely difficult.

But MacArthur prevailed. On September 15 Operation CHROMITE began. Under the cover of intense naval and air bombardment, U.S. Marines quickly took the port of Inchon. Within a few days, UN forces had recaptured Seoul and returned Rhee to the capital.

While Inchon was falling, the soldiers defending the Pusan Perimeter staged a massive offensive that finally broke through the surrounding North Korean line. Caught between MacArthur's forces in the north and the UN troops advancing from Pusan, the enemy began its retreat. Thousands of North Korean soldiers surrendered or escaped through the mountains. By September 30, the North Korean army was finally pushed back across the 38th Parallel. After three months of bloody fighting, it seemed the war might be over. But the politicians had other ideas.

Rhee and UN secretary-general Trygve Lie (pronounced TRIG-ve Lee) had long hoped for a unified Korea. MacArthur, too, was anxious to push farther north. So the UN granted MacArthur permission to advance his troops into North Korea. Some thought that such a move would bring communist China

THEY WENT TO WAR

Nearly six million Americans served in some capacity during the Korean War. The following branches of our armed forces were represented in the United Nations effort to restore peace in Korea.

Troops from Thailand arrive at Inchon in January 1953. Twenty-two nations participated in the UN-led effort to help South Korea.

U.S. Army
    8th U.S. Army
    I Corps
    IX Corps
    X Corps

U.S. Army Reserve

U.S. Army National Guard

U.S. Navy
    Task Force 77 (7th Fleet Striking Force)
    Military Sea Transportation Service
    Seabees (Construction Battalion)

U.S. Marine Corps
    1st Provisional Marine Brigade
    1st Marine Division
    1st Marine Aircraft Wing

U.S. Marine Corps Reserve

U.S. Air Force
    5th Air Force
    Military Air Transport Service
    Combat Cargo Command

U.S. Air Force Reserve

Air National Guard

U.S. Coast Guard — C.E.B.

into the war. Others feared that it might even start another world war. But MacArthur dismissed these concerns, telling President Truman that there was "very little" chance of Chinese involvement.

As UN troops marched into North Korea and headed toward the Yalu River, the border between China and North Korea, more than 100,000 experienced Chinese soldiers were slipping across the river. On November 25, the Chinese attacked. Two days later, UN and Chinese troops clashed at the Changjin (Chosin) Reservoir, in northeast Korea. A massive Chinese assault forced a UN retreat toward the port of Hungnam. Fighting bitter cold all the way to Hungnam, nearly 200,000 UN troops and Korean refugees, as well as thousands of military vehicles, were eventually evacuated by sea on U.S. Navy ships and merchant vessels.

Throughout the winter and into the spring, the war dragged on. On July 10, 1951, peace talks began in

Seoul, South Korea, was invaded several times by North Korean troops. Here you can see the dome of the capitol building in the background, but other parts of the city were destroyed.

Kaesong, North Korea. But for the next two years, fighting continued along a relatively stationary battle-front near the 38th Parallel. Bloody battles were waged for control of strategic areas with unusual names: Heartbreak Ridge, Old Baldy, Pork Chop Hill. American F-86 Sabre jets battled Soviet-made MiG-15 fighters in "MiG Alley," an area over north-west North Korea just south of the Yalu River. Forty U.S. pilots became "aces," each downing at least five enemy planes.

In the late spring of 1953, peace negotiators finally agreed on all major points. On July 27, artillery fire along the front slowed, then ceased. Machine guns and then rifles soon grew quiet. At 10:00 P.M., a long-awaited silence descended on the rugged battlefield. The Korean War was over.

Craig E. Blohm has written and edited several social studies textbooks and is a frequent contributor to *COBBLESTONE, CALLIOPE,* and *ODYSSEY.*

BELOW: Marines on patrol surround a hut as they search for enemy soldiers. Note the feet of a man lying in the doorway. RIGHT: All military personnel were issued dog tags to serve as a form of identification. They included the bearer's name, serial number, blood type, religion, and year he or she entered the service.

SEPTEMBER 15–16, 1950

U.S. forces land at Inchon.

SEPTEMBER 16–22, 1950

UN forces break out of Pusan Perimeter, attack north, and recapture Seoul.

JANUARY–APRIL 1951

Chinese army pushes UN forces back across the 38th Parallel and recaptures Seoul.

JUNE 25, 1950

With the 38th Parallel crossing, North Korea invades South Korea.

MAY 1951

UN counterattack frees Seoul. Fighting stalls around the 38th Parallel.

NOVEMBER 25, 1950

Chinese army enters North Korea and pushes UN forces back from the Yalu River.

JUNE 28, 1950

Seoul, South Korea's capital, is captured by communist forces. U.S. and South Korean forces retreat southward.

JUNE 1951– JULY 1953

UN and communist forces fight sporadic battles for control of territory around the 38th Parallel.

NOVEMBER 27–28, 1950

UN forces are surrounded at the Changjin (Chosin) Reservoir.

AUGUST 4– SEPTEMBER 16, 1950

U.S. and South Korean troops establish a defensive perimeter around Pusan. North Korean advance is stopped.

JULY 10, 1951

Peace talks begin at Kaesong and eventually continue at Panmunjom.

DECEMBER 9–24, 1950

Evacuation of UN forces from port city of Hungnam.

1950

1951

1952

The 50th Anniversary of the Korean War

Commemoration Committee

has developed a variety of educational materials for use in the classroom. Schools can order these materials free of charge by completing this card and mailing it.

Name _____

School _____

Address _____

City _____

State _____ Zip _____

Visit our Web site: http://Korea50.army.mil

**50th Aniversary of the Korean War
Commemoration Committee**
**1213 Jefferson Davis Highway
Crystal Gateway 4, Suite 702
Arlington, VA 22202-4303**

IｌｌｄｌｌｌｌｌｌＩＩＩｌｌＩＩＩｌｌｌｌｌｌＩＩｌｌｌＩＩＩｌｌｌｌｌＩＩＩｌ

Time Line
OF IMPORTANT DATES

The Korean War involved air (TOP LEFT), land (ABOVE LEFT and RIGHT), and sea (ABOVE) manpower and machinery provided by the United Nations. U.S. general Douglas MacArthur (LEFT) was the first supreme commander of these forces.

JULY 27, 1953
Armistice temporarily ends fighting. A permanent peace treaty is never signed.

1953

1954

THE BIG

by Craig

President Harry S. Truman

As president of the United States during most of the Korean War, Truman authorized sending American troops to Korea. He never asked Congress for a declaration of war, however, instead referring to U.S. involvement in Korea as a "police action."

President Dwight D. Eisenhower

"I shall go to Korea," Eisenhower declared in his 1951 presidential campaign. He kept his promise in December 1952, visiting the troops (including his son, John) and meeting with South Korean president Syngman Rhee. Eisenhower was president when the armistice was signed in 1953.

President Syngman Rhee

Educated in the United States, Rhee was elected the Republic of Korea's first president at age seventy-three. A firm believer in Korean unity, he tried to stall the peace talks in hopes of reuniting the country. Although Rhee finally agreed to the war's end, he never accepted the armistice conditions.

General Douglas MacArthur

As supreme commander of the United Nations (UN) forces in Korea, MacArthur devised the brilliant and successful invasion of Inchon. Because of controversial public statements about the war, however, he was relieved of his command in April 1951.

General Paik Sun Yup

Paik commanded the South Korean army's 1st Division, which captured the North Korean capital of Pyongyang, Paik's hometown. Later named chief of staff, he took part in the peace negotiations in Panmunjom.

illustrated by Patrick M. Reynolds

PLAYERS

Premier Kim Il Sung

Kim joined the Communist party in 1931, receiving military training in the Soviet Union. He was appointed premier of the Democratic People's Republic of Korea (North Korea) in 1948 and was the guiding force behind the invasion of South Korea.

Premier Joseph Stalin

A ruthless dictator, Stalin ruled the Soviet Union with an iron hand, making it a world power. He agreed to Kim's plan to invade South Korea and later convinced communist China to enter the war.

Chairman Mao Zedong

Mao was the leader of communist China from 1949 until his death in 1976. Fearing the collapse of North Korea, and with the backing of the Soviet Union, Mao sent Chinese soldiers across the Yalu River to fight against UN forces in 1950.

General Matthew B. Ridgway

An experienced World War II veteran, Ridgway commanded the U.S. 8th Army in Korea. He led the 8th Army in turning back the Chinese advance in early 1951 and later succeeded MacArthur as commander of UN forces in Korea.

General Mark Clark

In May 1952, Clark succeeded Ridgway as commander of UN forces in Korea. He served in this capacity through the end of the difficult peace negotiations and later wrote two books about his war experiences.

Secretary-General Trygve Lie

Lie, the first secretary-general of the UN, called for world action against North Korea for its attack on South Korea. Under mounting criticism from the Soviet Union, he resigned from the UN in April 1953.

19

Patrick M. Reynolds

Two Years OF TALKING

by Kathiann M. Kowalski

By June 1951, the Korean War was at a *stalemate.* United Nations (UN) forces had pushed back the Communists and gained ground. (See the time line on page 16 for specific troop movements.) But they could not win the war without losing many more lives.

Then Yakov Malik, Soviet delegate to the UN, hinted that North Korea was ready to discuss an *armistice.* General Matthew B. Ridgway suggested meeting aboard the Danish hospital ship *Jutlandia,* moored off Korea's coast. North Korea agreed to talk — but at Kaesong, in communist territory.

On July 10, 1951, UN negotiators arrived in Kaesong, three miles south of the 38th Parallel. U.S. vice admiral C. Turner Joy headed the delegation. Korean general Nam Il was named senior delegate for the Communists. In reality, however, Chinese general Hsieh Fang held the most authority.

The talks began badly. "At the first meeting of the delegates, I seated myself at the conference table and almost sank out of sight," Joy recalled. His unusually short chair made Nam seem tall across the table — a not-so-subtle attempt by the Communists to show their superiority. Joy switched chairs.

Just agreeing on what to discuss took ten days. The in-depth talks were even more difficult. For instance, there was disagreement about where North and South Korea should be divided during an armistice. The Communists insisted on the 38th Parallel, but that line was hard to defend from a military standpoint. By July 1951, UN troops had pushed north of the 38th Parallel in most places. Joy refused to give back what North Korea had lost on the battlefield.

ABOVE and BELOW: Discussions to end the war did not mean the fighting stopped. UN forces continued to bomb North Korea, as captured in this photo dated July 13, 1951. RIGHT: Former UN prisoners of war warm themselves around a stove after being released by the Chinese. How to handle prisoners of war became an important issue during the peace talks.

Each side accused the other of bad faith and delay. One day, both sides got so angry that the delegates sat in stony silence for more than two hours.

While the negotiators worked, UN forces applied pressure on the battlefield. But because U.S. policymakers would not allow all-out war, bat-

tles were sporadic. The Communists applied pressure, too, especially with propaganda. At one point, they falsely accused the UN of bombing Kaesong. The talks broke off.

When the negotiations resumed, delegates met at Panmunjom, in neutral territory. Within a month, they agreed to a *demarcation* line along battle lines. The cease-fire issue came next.

A demarcation is a line used to designate two distinct areas.

21

Indian troops were assigned to guard the Chinese and North Korean prisoners of war who did not want to be sent back to their Communist-led countries.

Saving face means avoiding shame or embarrassment.

Repatriation means the return of a prisoner of war to his or her country of citizenship.

The UN did not want the Communists building up forces during an armistice. Similarly, the Communists wanted to deplete UN forces by hindering troop rotations. Both sides agreed that having neutral nations police any cease-fire was the best option. Then the Communists proposed that the Soviet Union oversee the cease-fire. Having supplied arms to North Korea, the Soviet Union was certainly not neutral. The Communists eventually conceded this point.

Throughout the negotiations, the Communists saw any concessions on their part as a sign of weakness. They hoped that delaying an agreement would wear down their opponents, and they placed top priority on *saving face.*

The thorniest problem was prisoners of war. Although the Communists listed more than ten thousand South Korean and UN prisoners, that was thousands fewer than they had previously announced capturing. The Communists never fully explained the discrepancy. Most likely, the "missing" prisoners had died.

By contrast, the UN held tens of thousands of North Korean and Chinese prisoners. Many of them did not want to return to their communist homelands, however. The debate over "no forced *repatriation*" continued for fourteen months after Lieutenant General William

Harrison replaced Joy as lead UN negotiator in May 1952.

International Red Cross appeals finally led to Operation Little Switch in April 1953. The Communists delivered fewer than one thousand sick or wounded prisoners to UN forces. The UN returned more than six thousand ill or injured communist troops.

The sides also agreed on Operation Big Switch. After the armistice went into effect, a commission from neutral countries would take custody of prisoners refusing repatriation. Their countries of origin could encourage them to return, but the prisoners would make the final decision. About 22,500 prisoners in UN custody ultimately refused to return to China and North Korea.

On July 27, 1953, Harrison and Nam signed the armistice, which was later signed by the commander of the UN forces, General Mark Clark. Because Korea remained divided, South Korea refused to sign. The war that had never officially been declared also never officially ended with a peace treaty. After two years of talks, the fighting finally stopped, but today Korea remains divided by a heavily guarded *demilitarized zone.*

Kathiann M. Kowalski is the author of several books and dozens of articles for young people. She lives in Fairview Park, Ohio, and is a frequent contributor to *COBBLESTONE* and *ODYSSEY*.

A demilitarized zone (DMZ) is an area where military forces and operations are prohibited.

After two years of negotiations, U.S. general Mark Clark signs an armistice on July 27, 1953. Vice Admiral Robert Briscoe and Vice Admiral J.J. Clark witness the event.

History's first all-jet air battle took place during the Korean War, when North Korean MiG-15s engaged U.S. F-80C's (Shooting Stars) on November 8, 1950.

The 38th Parallel is not a physical barrier. It is a line of latitude, and the demilitarized zone around it in Korea — consisting of a mile-wide area that extends across 487 square miles — continues to be the focus of military attention today.

The name "Korea" comes from the historical Koryo Kingdom (918-1392). The more poetic "Land of the Morning Calm" (Choson in Korean) was coined by the Koreans themselves. It refers to the beautiful and calm scenery found in the mountains in the eastern part of the country.

Did You Know?

Women in the Korean Women's Army fought on the frontlines with their fathers and brothers during the Korean War.

Hey, Sis! Mom wants to know if you'll be home for dinner tonight!!

Rather than being taken in by force, many Communists surrendered to UN troops after reading propagandist leaflets distributed by the United Nations.

President Harry S. Truman referred to the Korean War as a "police action." He committed U.S. troops to South Korea without the approval of Congress, which is the branch of government with the sole authority to declare war.

RELIEF FOR REFUGEES

Humanitarian Work in the Korean War

by Stephen Currie

This photo captures the crowded deck of the SS Meredith Victory, which helped evacuate an estimated 14,000 refugees from Hungnam in December 1950.

Refugees are people who flee their homes in search of protection in times of war or political or religious oppression.

The Korean War caused widespread suffering among civilians as well as among soldiers. With war raging across the Korean peninsula, no place was safe. Families abandoned their homes when armies came near, and those who stayed often had to leave at gunpoint. Bombs destroyed schools, hospitals, and houses in addition to military targets. Korean cities overflowed with *refugees* from the countryside. Other refugees crowded into camps, where they lived in makeshift tents or huts and waited to return home.

Homelessness was not the only problem. Many food supplies were destroyed, and those that remained often did not reach the neediest Koreans. In some camps, people received only a handful or two of rice a day. Refugees usually left home with little more than the clothes they were wearing, so clothing soon became an issue, too. Worse, refugees caught *tuberculosis* and other diseases that swept through the cities and camps. Many died. At one point during the war, there were 100,000 orphans in South Korea alone. The situation was desperate.

But there was hope for the refugees. Individuals and organizations around the world decided to help. Money and supplies poured into Korea from the United States, Venezuela, Australia, and many other nations. These humanitarian, or relief, efforts were the difference between life and death for many Korean refugees.

Relief took various forms. Some groups collected supplies to help the refugees. Many of these drives were run by large organizations, with one international aid group gathering more than a million blankets. But smaller groups and individuals were at the heart of this relief effort. New York City schoolchildren donated mittens to keep refugees warm during the winter. A group calling itself Knit

for Korea urged women to make clothing to send overseas. And a "relief train" crossed the United States, collecting soap, shoes, and other supplies from Americans.

Businesses and governments sent supplies as well. A chemical company donated *penicillin,* and garment manufacturers provided boxes of new clothing. Germany supplied medical equipment. Pakistan sent five thousand tons of wheat. Liberia offered the United

Tuberculosis is an infectious disease of the lungs.

Penicillin is a drug used in the treatment of a number of diseases and infections.

War often involves innocent victims. This Korean girl was photographed crying in the street after a battle between U.S. Marines and North Korean forces around Inchon.

Nations several tons of rubber if that would help; the gift was accepted.

Aid also came in the form of money. Sometimes it made more sense for relief workers to buy medicine, food, or building supplies than to collect them. Organizations such as the International Red Cross earmarked millions of dollars to help Korean War refugees. Much of the money had been donated by ordinary people across the world. Some governments contributed, too. Canada, for instance, donated more than seven million dollars in 1951. Aid workers spent the donated money in ways they thought would do the most good.

Still another way to help was action. The Red Cross sent doctors and nurses to refugee camps, where they performed surgery, distributed medicine, and vaccinated people against the most common diseases. A religious organization called for volunteers to rebuild hospitals and schools. Several ships, including the Norwegian freighter *Reinholt* and the U.S. Merchant Marine ship *Meredith Victory*, transported refugees and others trapped by fighting. Some Americans even adopted war orphans. A Michigan couple received national attention for taking in two Korean orphans, and a Navy man brought home an orphan he had met while on active duty.

Not all relief efforts were successful. Money was sometimes badly managed. Donated supplies were not always suitable, and both sides occasionally prevented shipments from going through. Still, humanitarian work did make a difference for many refugees. These efforts were one of the few bright spots in a terrible and tragic war. 🎇

A soldier helps a Korean boy find the "perfect" pair of pants. The Marine Corps League of the United States distributed clothing and toys to South Koreans.

Stephen Currie is a history writer and teacher who lives in Poughkeepsie, New York.

WOMEN
IN THE WAR

by Ruth Tenzer Feldman

On June 26, 1950, while Captain Viola McConnell helped hundreds of people leave Korea, Marguerite Higgins fought to stay.

When war broke out, twenty-six-year-old McConnell was the only Army nurse stationed in Korea. Assigned to help evacuate Americans there, she treated nearly seven hundred people sailing aboard a freighter built to hold twelve passengers. (The crew gave up their quarters to babies and young children, while other passengers were given blankets to sleep in the hold of the ship.) McConnell worked without sleep for the two-day trip to Japan. She found several people with medical training among the passengers. Together, they cared for a person with a fractured skull, three women ready to give birth, a baby with pneumonia, and others with illnesses or injuries.

Twenty-nine-year-old Higgins was the only female American reporter in Korea. At the start of the war, she hitched a ride to

Korean War nurses often worked under difficult conditions. Here Captain Irene Wiley prepares medicine for a patient on board an air evacuation plane.

Two nurses prepare for incoming wounded at a Mobile Army Surgical Hospital (MASH) unit by inspecting litters stacked outside the hospital.

the frontlines. Then she flew to Japan to file her story with her newspaper, the *New York Herald.* When Higgins returned to Korea, a colonel told her, "You'll have to go right back, young lady. You can't stay here. There may be trouble."

"Trouble is news and gathering the news is my job," she replied.

The head of American forces in Korea banned Higgins from the war zone, and military policemen put her on an air-

plane to Japan. There she convinced General Douglas MacArthur to let her return. Higgins traveled in Korea with her essentials — a toothbrush, a box of flea powder, and a typewriter. She tried to stay close to battle. "If you worried about being shot at," she wrote, "you'd never get a story."

McConnell and Higgins were among the many American women in Korea during the war. Most were military nurses who had been in World War II.

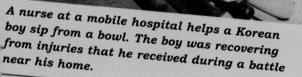

As assistant secretary of defense for manpower and personnel, Anna Rosenberg traveled to Korea and worked to integrate more women into the armed forces.

A nurse at a mobile hospital helps a Korean boy sip from a bowl. The boy was recovering from injuries that he received during a battle near his home.

All were volunteers. About 540 members of the Army Nurse Corps served in 25 medical facilities, from station hospitals to Mobile Army Surgical Hospital (MASH) units. Living conditions for the nurses were usually the same as those for the rest of the troops.

Air Force nurses assisted in air evacuations to hospitals in Japan. By July 1953, Air Force nurses had helped evacuate about 350,000 people. Navy nurses served on hospital ships, which, like MASH units, often followed the battle lines. Like Air Force nurses, they gave more than medical care. For example, while sailing with four hundred patients on Christmas Eve, 1950, nurses of the 121 Evacuation Hospital "had Christmas for everyone,...a tree, Santa Claus,... and a dance in the Operating Room." Navy nurses Estelle Kalnoske Lange and Ruth Cohen received the Bronze Star for their efforts.

During the Korean War, about forty-nine thousand women were in the U.S. armed services, including women in various medical corps, the Women's Army Corps (WAC), Women in the Air Force (WAF), the Navy's Women Accepted for Volunteer Emergency Service (Waves), and Women Marines. Many had duties involving health care and administration. Some were electronic technicians, radio operators, and **cryptographers.** Since women were not allowed to serve in combat positions, most were stationed outside Korea. Seven WACs did, however, serve in support positions in Korea.

By 1951, there was a serious shortage of nurses in Korea. Nurse anesthetists such as Katherine Wilson had to serve as many as six operating tables at once, until they were nearly anesthetized themselves from the fumes. Shortages of Army women were so great that a group of WACs were recalled from the reserves into active duty. This was the first time women were summoned to military duty rather than volun-

A **cryptographer** is a person who uses or develops a secret cipher, or coding system.

H*O*S*P*I*T*A*L*S
ON THE MOVE

During the Korean War, the Army used Mobile Army Surgical Hospital (MASH) units, which moved with the troops. These units were intended to provide emergency surgery for soldiers, who were then transported to better-equipped facilities away from the battlefield. However, MASH units soon became small, all-purpose hospitals. Designed to care for at most sixty patients, they often were swamped with hundreds of soldiers and civilians.

Helicopters played an important role in wartime medical care by evacuating wounded soldiers to and from

Imagine how frightening it must have been to be injured, loaded onto an exposed litter attached to a helicopter, and then evacuated to a hospital behind the lines.

Cobblestone Publishing Company
30 Grove Street, Suite C
Peterborough, NH 03458-1454

Ill␣␣␣Il␣I␣I␣I␣I␣I␣I␣I␣I␣␣␣IlI␣I␣I␣I␣I␣I␣IlI␣I

teering for it.

Anna Rosenberg, assistant secretary of defense for manpower and personnel, sought to increase the number of women in the military and better integrate them into the armed forces. In 1951, she formed the Defense Advisory Committee on Women in the Services (DACOWITS). The committee, which included many prominent women, undertook a massive recruitment campaign. Famous actresses such as Helen Hayes lent their support. DACOWITS brought many women into the military and still exists today.

Some women in the Korean War earned special recognition. Viola McConnell, for example, was awarded the Bronze Star for her evacuation work. Marguerite Higgins was awarded the Pulitzer Prize for international reporting. In doing their jobs, these women paved the way for better opportunities for women in the military and the workplace.

Ruth Tenzer Feldman is an author and frequent contributor to *COBBLESTONE* and *ODYSSEY*.

MASH units. Although relatively few patients were moved this way, helicopters helped save many lives.

During the Chinese invasion in late 1950, MASH units often moved every few days. Working in bitter cold operating tents, doctors and medical technicians learned combat medicine on the job. *Plasma* froze, generator fuel lines were clogged with ice, and surgeons worked by flashlight.

You may have seen reruns of the popular television show *M*A*S*H* (1972–1983). Were the real MASH units anything like the one portrayed in this series? Luluah Houseknecht was a nurse in the 8055 MASH unit in 1950. "We never had time to do all the playing they did on TV," she said. "If we weren't busy taking care of the patients, we were packing up and moving on." By 1952, however, many MASH units moved only two or three times a year.

Dora Stohl was head of the postoperative ward of the 8055 MASH unit in 1953, when it was on the 38th Parallel. It was in the same location as the fictional 4077 MASH unit in the TV series. She lived in a tent with cots in three corners and a place for refreshments in the fourth. "The TV series is true to the life and times of our unit," Stohl recalled, "and I am especially fond of the cease-fire...episode, which is exactly as it happened...in July of 1953." — **R.T.F.**

> **Plasma is the clear, yellowish portion of blood.**

MACHINE CODE

by Ruth Tenzer Feldman

During the Korean War, the U.S. armed services used machines to encode and decode messages. Here's a way to make your own very simple machine that makes hundreds of different codes. It's an Alberti disk, named for the Italian architect Leon Battista Alberti, who first used it in the 1400s.

You Need

two cardboard disks or paper plates, one smaller than the other

pen

paper fastener

1. Write the alphabet from A to Z on the rim of the smaller disk. Make sure the letters are spaced evenly around the disk.
2. Attach the smaller disk to the larger disk with a paper fastener through the centers of both disks. Write the alphabet in random order along the edge of the larger disk, so that each letter lines up with a letter on the smaller disk.
3. To encode a message, turn the disk until whatever letter you want on the larger disk is above the A on the smaller disk. Then keep the disks still and encode your message, substituting the letters on the larger disk for the corresponding letters on the smaller disk. For example, using the Alberti disk printed here, with W on the larger disk lined up with A on the smaller disk, "war" becomes "own."

If you want to make your code harder, work out a pattern between the letters or words you are encoding, as if the disk were a combination lock. For example, after encoding your first letter or word, turn the smaller disk three letters to the left and encode your second letter or word. Then move the smaller disk six letters to the right, and so forth.

34   illustrated by Peter Bono

4. Make an identical Alberti disk for your decoding buddy, or lend him or her your disk. Tell your friend which letter you picked to match *A* on the smaller disk and any "combination" you used. Your coding machine is ready to roll!

This month's quote is taken from the Korean War Veterans Memorial in Washington, D.C. The quote comes from a statement by the U.S. secretary of defense in 1988, on the thirty-fifth anniversary of the armistice. Using the Alberti disk printed here, decode the quote and the name of its author. Answer on page 48.

"Our nation honors her sons and daughters who answered the call to JBRBHJ W DGTHUNV UCBV HBEBN SHBO WHJ W LBGLKB UCBV HBEBN YBU."

— RNWHS DWNKTDDQ

Integrating the Armed Forces

by Sylvia Whitman

During the Korean War, black and white U.S. soldiers fought side by side in an armed conflict for the first time.

African Americans helped the United States win World War II. They worked in factories that produced guns, tanks, and battleships. They fought and died overseas. But when the war ended in 1945, the country they had served still treated them as second-class citizens. In 1946, for instance, a white mob in Georgia shot and killed two African American married couples, including a veteran. What had happened to that spirit of wartime unity, African Americans wondered, and the

concept of liberty and justice for all?

Troubled by violent incidents and pressured by black leaders and voters, President Harry S. Truman ended some forms of discrimination in the military. Like most of American society, the military operated under a policy of "separate but equal." African Americans were given separate facilities (such as restrooms) that were supposed to be of the same quality as those given to whites. Black facilities were often of inferior quality, however.

Segregation in the military made African Americans feel like second-rate soldiers and sailors. Often they were assigned to support units as truck drivers or cooks. They found few avenues for promotion and leadership. In 1948, President Truman signed Executive Order 9981, which called for "equality of treatment and opportunity for all persons in the Armed Forces."

Although Truman ordered quick change, the military did not respond swiftly. Even if officers claimed to have no racial prejudice, they argued that white troops would refuse to eat, sleep, train, and fight with

In 1948, President Harry S. Truman signed Executive Order 9981, which marked the official end of segregation in the armed forces.

African Americans and would disobey black officers. By the time the Korean War began, the Air Force had integrated its ranks, but the Army and Navy lagged behind.

Stationed in Japan, the Army's only all-black regiment, the 24th Infantry, arrived in Korea soon after the North invaded the South. Within weeks, one of its battalions drove the North Koreans out of the crossroads town of Yechon. The thrill of this small victory did not last, however. Like other American regiments, the 24th Infantry had grown soft during occupation duty in Japan. These troops had not trained for night combat. They also struggled with old equipment and poor maps. But the 24th Infantry had an even bigger problem: lack of trust between black soldiers and white officers.

For years, racial tension had been nibbling away at the regi-

ment's effectiveness. White officers cycled through the 24th Infantry, rarely staying long enough to develop a solid relationship with the men. Prejudice took many forms, from low expectations to insults. In that first muggy summer in Korea, morale hit bottom. Many Americans "bugged out" (ran away instead of firing back at the enemy) in Korea, but the 24th Infantry became especially notorious for quitting posts. White commanders blamed combat disasters on "incompetent" black troops — never on their own lack of leadership. In September, the major general overseeing the 24th Infantry recommended that it be disbanded as "untrustworthy and incapable of carrying out missions."

Meanwhile, Army leaders back home tried desegregation to offset a shortage of white recruits. The Army had plenty of black recruits and decided to begin filling holes in white units with African American soldiers. A study of a few integrated units showed that the blacks in these units performed as well as the whites. Another report focused on the efficiency of operating one personnel system instead of two separate ones.

In 1951, General Matthew B. Ridgway asked for and received permission to end segregation in the Army. Some units, such as the 24th Infantry, were dissolved, while others added white or black troops to achieve a mix. By October 1953, the Army had integrated ninety-five percent of its troops.

During the Korean War, the number of black soldiers and officers more than quadrupled. The Navy took longer to integrate, but the drive for efficiency turned the Army into an unlikely civil rights leader. 🎆

Sylvia Whitman is a writer who lives in Orlando, Florida. She has written several children's books.

African American soldiers of the 24th Infantry Regiment are being sent up to the battlefront in July 1950.

Heroes of Many Hues

The nation's highest military award, the Congressional Medal of Honor, recognizes outstanding valor (courage) in battle. It was introduced during the Civil War. Early recipients included black soldiers who fought for the Union. By the end of World War II, the Medal of Honor was presented to 440 veterans — not one of them black.

After the Korean War, heroes from many ethnic backgrounds received the Medal of Honor. These included Hispanic Americans, Asian Americans, and one Native American, Mitchell Red Cloud, Jr. The two African American recipients, William Thompson and Cornelius Charlton, served in the all-black 24th Infantry Regiment. Jesse Brown, the Navy's first African American combat pilot, received the Distinguished Flying Cross.

The two African American Medal of Honor recipients died in combat. On August 6, 1950, North Koreans surprised Private William Thompson's platoon after dark. Thompson "set up his machinegun in the path of the onslaught and swept the enemy with withering fire," according to his citation. He halted the attack long enough for the Americans to scramble to better positions. "He resisted all efforts of his comrades to induce him to withdraw, steadfastly remained at his machinegun and continued to deliver deadly, accurate fire until mortally wounded." His "dauntless courage and gallant self-sacrifice reflect the highest credit on himself."

On June 2, 1951, Sergeant Cornelius Charlton took command after his platoon leader was wounded. He led three charges up a heavily defended hill and was wounded in the chest, but he continued charging and firing, single-handedly chasing out the enemy, who lobbed a grenade at him. He died of his wounds. His parents accepted the Medal of Honor on his behalf. — **S.W.**

The Congressional Medal of Honor is the highest military award presented in the United States. It goes to those who perform outstanding acts of courage in battle.

A Korean War Crossword Puzzle

by Meg Chorlian

The crossword puzzle on these pages consists of some of the important people, places, and events that relate to the Korean War. All the answers to the puzzle appear somewhere in this issue. Answers on page 48.

ACROSS

1. For two years, fighting during the war stalled around the 38th _____.
5. These mobile hospital units were made famous by a television series.
6. North Korea received aid from China and the _____ _____.
7. This half of Korea is also known as the Republic of Korea.
11. Anna _____ was the assistant secretary of defense for manpower and personnel during the war.
13. This river border between China and North Korea was threatened by UN troops in the fall of 1950.
15. The Korean War was the first war in which African Americans were _____ into fighting units in the Army.
16. The Korean War is often referred to as the _____ _____.
17. Syngman _____ was the president of the Republic of Korea.
18. _____ Il Sung was the premier of the Democratic People's Republic of Korea.
19. As thousands of Koreans became _____, they were the focus of international humanitarian efforts.
20. This is the capital of South Korea.

DOWN

2. In April 1953, Operation
   ____ ____ was the first
   attempt to address the
   difficult issue of how to
   handle prisoners of war.
3. The first round of peace
   talks took place in this
   North Korean city.
4. This port city in South
   Korea became the famous
   landing site of UN troops
   in September 1950.
8. On July 27, 1953, this
   was signed to end the
   fighting.
9. General Douglas ____
   was the supreme com-
   mander of UN forces
   until April 1951.
10. UN troops held this
    defensive perimeter in
    South Korea.
12. General Matthew B.
    ____ succeeded
    MacArthur as UN
    commander.
14. Marguerite ____ was the
    only female American
    reporter in Korea.

These American F-86 Sabre jets prepare to leave for
"MiG Alley" in search of Soviet-built MiG-15s.

An Interview with a Korean War Veteran

by Meg Chorlian

As a 17-year-old, Harley Coon enlisted in the U.S. Army in 1948 to help fight the Soviets.

In September 1948, seventeen-year-old Harley Coon enlisted in the U.S. Army. At that time (following World War II), the Soviet Union was the enemy of the United States, and soldiers were motivated to join the Army to fight the Soviets. Coon was assigned to the 25th Infantry and arrived in Korea in June 1950. Whereas most soldiers served for one year, he served for more than three years (thirty-eight months). He spent more than thirty-three months as a prisoner of war (POW). COBBLESTONE had the privilege of speaking with Coon about his Korean War experience.

Did you see active fighting?

Within a day of arriving in Korea, we went into combat. We were sent to help free some soldiers from a trap, but we couldn't get to

This photograph of a clearly happy Harley Coon was taken on August 31, 1953. It was the day after he was released from the prisoner of war camp as part of Operation Big Switch.

them. I spent five months on the frontline before we were overrun by the Chinese on November 27, 1950, at Chosin.

What was it like to be in combat?

Frightening a lot of the time. People who say otherwise are not in their right minds. While we were fighting, there was not much time to think about it. Only afterward would we think about what could have happened.

You were captured by the Chinese. What was your POW experience like?

In the first eight months of my

captivity, there were 100 to 150 prisoners dying each day. Of the 230 men in my group, 6 survived the war. The North Koreans and Chinese did not honor the Geneva conventions [a series of guidelines for the humane treatment of POWs]. I spent one year in the same clothes — no showers, no haircuts, no opportunity to shave. From November 27, 1950, to June or July 1951, I was unable to bathe. We were finally permitted to bathe when we were in a position near the Yalu River.

Is it difficult for you to talk about your POW experience?

Yes. For the first twenty-five to thirty years, I wouldn't talk about it. Then I went to a history presentation where every war but the Korean War was mentioned. That irritated me. I asked the professor why, and he told me that it had been a police action. Then my granddaughter asked me to talk to her third-grade class. I started to talk about my experience to audiences that ranged from third-graders to college students.

basic freedoms, and American soldiers are willing to put their lives on the line to protect their loved ones. It is the supreme sacrifice. We pay a great price to keep those freedoms. It is only after you lose your freedom that you realize what you had but never appreciated.

What do you think of the Korean War Veterans Memorial in Washington, D.C.?

It's beautiful — very, very impressive. The faces on the statues reflect all the emotions a soldier might feel — fear, anxiety, confusion. And then the wall nearby reflects all the branches of the armed services. It's awesome.

Have you ever returned to Korea?

I've been there four times. The first time I went back was in 1985. It was very emotional. I was trying to find a hill we had nicknamed "C Ration Hill". We would throw our rations down the hill, and the enemy would trip over them and make noise. Then we'd open fire. We had flares and barbed wire set up, but the noise of the rations worked better. The enemy didn't expect that.

What should young people today understand about the Korean War?

It's not only about Korea — it's true for all wars. Americans have

The Korean War left Harley Coon with a permanent disability. Today he lives in Beavercreek, Ohio, with his wife, Sylvia. He has three children and five grandchildren. Although he is retired, he is the national president of the Korean War Veterans Association. The job requires international travel to represent the association, which strives to keep the memory of the "Forgotten War" alive. "We want people to understand that the war may have ended in a tie, but it represented the beginning of the end of the spread of communism," Coon says.

Brain Ticklers

Give your brain a little tickle to see how well you read and understood this issue commemorating the Korean War. If you believe the answer to be false, give yourself the ultimate test and see whether you can explain why it is false. Answers on page 48.

1. The opposing sides engaged in three years of intense fighting during the Korean War.
   ☐ True   ☐ False

2. One of the primary causes of the Korean War was a basic distrust between the United States and the Soviet Union.
   ☐ True   ☐ False

3. General Douglas MacArthur led a strategic landing of UN forces at Kaesong, in North Korea.
   ☐ True   ☐ False

4. Prisoners of war were quickly returned to their respective countries while the armistice was being discussed.
   ☐ True   ☐ False

5. Though not permitted to serve as combat soldiers, American women filled important roles as nurses.
   ☐ True   ☐ False

6. The Korean War was the first conflict in which African Americans fought in the same regiments as white soldiers and officers in the U.S. Army.
   ☐ True   ☐ False

7. Fighting around the Changjin (Chosin) Reservoir resulted in a military victory for UN forces.
   ☐ True   ☐ False

A Final Word

Compare two slogans that have been used in reference to the Korean War: "Never Forgotten" and "Freedom Is Not Free." Which one sends a stronger message? Why do you think Korean War veterans prefer the second slogan?

Digging Deeper

Books to Read

Peacebound Trains by Haemi Balgassi (New York: Clarion Books, 1996) is a fictional account of a South Korean family's escape from Seoul during the Korean War. Grade 3 and up.

The Korean War by Carter Smith (Parsippany, New Jersey: Silver Burdett Press, 1990) is a book in the Turning Points in American History series that provides an introduction to the causes and events of the Korean War. Grade 5 and up.

For Older Readers

The Forgotten War: America in Korea, 1950–1953 by Clay Blair (New York: Random House, 1987).

Historical Dictionary of the Korean War edited by James I. Matray (Westport, Connecticut: Greenwood Press, 1991).

The Korean War: An Encyclopedia edited by Stanley Sandler (New York: Garland Publishers, 1995).

The Korean War: An International History by William Stueck (Princeton, New Jersey: Princeton University Press, 1995).

More Media

Resource materials are available from the **50th Anniversary of the Korean War Commemoration Committee.** Items include commemorative flags, posters, bookmarks, historical fact sheets, newsletters, certificates, and other memorabilia. Please write to 50th Anniversary of the Korean War Commemoration Committee, 1213 Jefferson Davis Highway, Crystal Gateway 4, Suite 702, Arlington, VA 22202. Include a note about how you plan to use the items.

Korean War Veterans Memorial, Washington, D.C. The memorial includes nineteen statues that reflect the diverse group of Americans who served in the war. There also is a mural that includes images of unnamed servicepeople and a pool for quiet reflection.

On the Web

The Department of Defense has a Web site that provides information about the commemoration of the Korean War: **korea50.army.mil**.

If you cannot travel to Washington, D.C., you can visit the Korean War Veterans Memorial on-line. Go to **www.nps.gov/kwvm/index2.htm** to read a brief history of the Korean War and a description of the memorial and how it was created.

To learn more about the relationship between South Korea and the United States, visit **www.koreasociety.org/**. It will connect you to the Korean Society Web site.

Interested in interviewing a Korean War veteran? By contacting the Veterans of Foreign Wars Web site at **www.vfw.org/home.shtml**, you can find some leads to locate veterans.

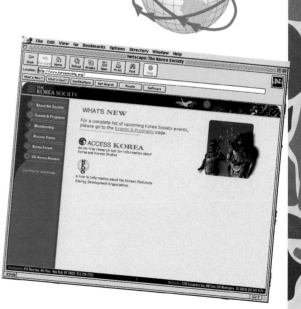

47

Third Division Infantrymen climb up the trail to their objective near Uijongbu, South Korea.

Answer to Quote of the Month: Machine Code from page 34.

"Our nation honors her sons and daughters who answered the call to defend a country they never knew and a people they never met."

— Frank Carlucci

Answers to A Korean War Crossword Puzzle from page 40.

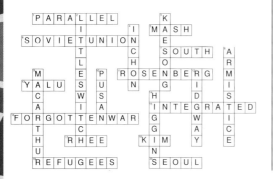

Answers to Brain Ticklers from page 45.

1. False. Only one-third of the war involved regular combat. The last two years saw minor battles while the two sides tried to negotiate a peaceful end to the war. **2. True. 3. False.** The UN forces landed at Inchon, in South Korea, and successfully pushed the invading North Korean army back over the 38th Parallel.

4. False. How to handle the thousands of prisoners of war was a sticky issue during the negotiations. Many North Korean and Chinese prisoners did not want to return to their native countries, and the UN refused to force them to return. **5. True. 6. True. 7. False.** UN troops were forced to retreat in the face of an overwhelming Chinese attack at Changjin. Ultimately, UN forces had to evacuate the area by sea.